THE ANCIENT GREEKS
AND THE
EVOLUTION OF
STANDARDS IN BUSINESS

THE ANCIENT GREEKS AND THE EVOLUTION OF STANDARDS IN BUSINESS

BY

GEORGE M. CALHOUN

BOSTON AND NEW YORK
HOUGHTON MIFFLIN COMPANY
The Riverside Press Cambridge
1926

The Riverside Press
CAMBRIDGE · MASSACHUSETTS
PRINTED IN THE U.S.A.

- The power has been transferred from the church or the state to the industry which means the burden of a big responsibility.

- The Phoenician were very tricky guys

- Conception of trade by the greeks.

- A new conception of trade: Hellas p.42

BARBARA WEINSTOCK
LECTURES ON THE MORALS
OF TRADE

This series will contain essays by
representative scholars and men of
affairs dealing with the various phases
of the moral law in its bearing on
business life under the new economic
order, first delivered at the University
of California on the Weinstock foundation.

THE ANCIENT GREEKS AND THE EVOLUTION OF STANDARDS IN BUSINESS

Most of us are aware that the modern world owes much to ancient Greece in the realms of art and literature, of philosophy and science. A few of us are beginning to realize that we have learned something from the Greeks of government and law — and could, if we would, learn more. But if I should tell you that these same Greeks made a substantial contribution to the development of the principles and practices which regulate the vast complexities of modern trade

and finance, the assertion would doubtless be hailed as the wildest paradox, and
credited to that unreasoning enthusiasm
with which the confirmed pedant re-
gards his own field of study and teaching. Permit me, therefore, to put my
subject in the form of a question to be
answered, rather than a thesis to be
maintained, and to speak to you, not as
an advocate of the glory that was Greece,
striving to add yet another leaf to her
crown of laurel, but as one who seeks
the solution of a fascinating problem.
What, if anything, have the ancient
Hellenes contributed to that long, slow
process of economic change and growth
which began ages before their time,
when some leading citizen of the Ne-

anderthal bartered flakes of flint with a neighbor for toothsome marrow bones?

I have said the problem is interesting. It is also important. The stately goddess Finance, with her two jewels Commerce and Industry, to-day rules over human destiny with a firmer sway than in any previous epoch; and the multifarious activities comprehended by the rather vague word 'business' absorb the time and energy of men to a greater degree than ever before. Not only the material comfort of the billions who populate the earth, but their intellectual and spiritual welfare as well, are directly conditioned by the operations of finance. The burden of responsibility that once rested mainly upon the leader of church or state has now been transferred in large part to the broad shoulders of the captain of industry.

In the interest of clarity it may be well to formulate explicitly what is implied in the word 'responsibility.' 'Business' in common with other occupations has its particular function; it has a purpose, to which its operations should be directed. This, I take it — and I speak diffidently, as a layman, in the presence of colleagues who have spent a lifetime in the study of these matters—is not the unreasoning production and distribution of wealth, but such production and distribution as will procure to mankind a maximum of material and spiritual well-being. This brings us, obviously, to the verge of an interminable philosophical disquisition, in which every term requires to be defined and given its proper relations. However, since I am not a philosopher or an economist, I may be permitted to cut the knot, and describe the function of business, somewhat loosely, as 'service,' its aim as the betterment of human life.

There is no need to observe that this is not a discovery of my own, for it is well-nigh a platitude. Among students of economics and ethics its validity has long been admitted, and it has recently been formulated with careful precision in an earlier lecture of this series. 'Service' is becoming a favorite 'slogan' in the world of trade; our business houses with one accord, from the leviathans of international finance to the plankton of retail merchandising, proclaim it as a new gospel. Here, however, are traces of misconception. Our men of affairs are inclined to feel that business, after long groping in the dark, has suddenly seen a great light; in the present trend of moral standards, which is undeniably upwards, they discern the beginnings of a spiritual revolution, a miraculous act of grace, destined to lead us in a short time into a commercial millennium, in which industry and trade will be the willing handmaids of a generous and noble culture. This feeling is splendid and inspiring and fraught with great possibilities for good.

Yet I must ask you to believe rather that we stand midway in a long, slow process of gradual evolution; that here, as in other departments of human activity, we are working but slowly toward the attainment of our larger ends. Much of the good we have is a heritage from remote predecessors, amassed bit by bit through long ages of time, and we cannot in this field disregard the past history of human experience any more than the sculptor or painter or architect or poet, who must constantly measure his work with that which has gone before.

The view that our economic history records a continuous evolution is not mere theory, or a speculative hypothesis formulated in the application of some abstract philosophy. It is a sober induction from a long array of facts, now become so complete, in consequence of recent discoveries, that the process may be sketched in its broader outlines with some assurance of scientific accuracy. As you well know, we can trace many of our own rules and practices through the commercial law of England to the usage of the communities that dominated Mediterranean trade in the Middle Ages; and from them to the Romans and to the mercantile law and custom of the ancient Hellenic world is but a step. But the Greeks in these matters were the pupils of their eastern neighbors, and so we go on, further and fur-

Summo-
rize of
the business
ethics
history.

ther back, through the Babylonian code of Hammurapi, to the forms and customs and the underlying rules of business that prevailed in the Sumerian city-states, three thousand years before the Christian era. And here we see the germ and essence of much that is valid and familiar to-day.

It is not surprising that the part of Greece in this tradition has received slight attention. We are a busy world, and the dollars that are piling up so fast must be counted and stowed—or flung—away. Much of this knowledge has been discovered but recently, and only very gradually is it coming to the notice of those who write economic history. But the most serious impediment to a just appreciation of the Hellenic contribution to economic progress lies in the preconceived ideas with which the subject is generally approached. Most of us get our notions of what an ancient Greek was like from the formalized scenes on Attic vases, from the sonorous verse of the great tragedians or the piquant extravaganza of Aristophanes, from the majestic calm of the Parthenon frieze or the stately beauty of a Platonic dialogue. Or perhaps we base our conception of the Greek business man upon a few scattered passages, relating to the cosmopolitan Greek of a later day, in which Latin authors give utterance to the bitter prejudice of the Romans, who were no better able to rival their elder brothers in the marts of trade than in the realm of art and letters. Thus, leaving aside the belief of Mr. Wells that the Hellenes were an unworthy rabble snarling at the heels of a tiny Periclean circle of pure and lofty souls, we have two manners of conceiving the ancient Greeks, quite incompatible with one another, and, in my opinion, equally remote from truth. The more usual is to shut our eyes to the evidence for their economic efficiency, and to picture them as brilliant visionaries, constantly preoccupied with eternal beauty and metaphysics, but deplorably impractical when confronted with the stern necessities of daily life. The other is to make them a race of clever, unscrupulous sharpers and swindlers, lacking even in the first principles of honesty and common decency. Although these two notions of the Hellenic character would seem to be mutually exclusive, we sometimes find them ingeniously combined in that queer sort of synthesis that goes to the making of textbooks. The idea—if it may be called an idea —seems to be something like this. The great majority of Greeks so hungered after the good, the true, and the beautiful that they lived constantly in the rarefied atmosphere of the intellectual and spiritual; when beset by material difficulties, they were hopelessly ineffective, but Providence watched over them and kept them from starving—possibly with an eye to the Renaissance. The little minority who preferred wealth to metaphysics or spiritual ecstasy were a frightful exemplification of the old maxim, *corruptio optimi pessima*, for they turned out to be the cleverest cheats and rascals of the ancient world.

To find out the truth, which obviously will lie somewhere between the two extremes, is not impossible, if we will but put away our preconceptions. In fact, we have only to remember that the ancient Greeks—and when we think of Greeks we inevitably think first of the Athenians—were living human beings, very human and very much alive, not wholly unlike ourselves. Athens was not alone the 'city of the violet crown,' 'the school of Hellas,' the abode of perfect beauty and the cradle of wisdom; she was also in her time the busy, bustling, pushing, 'boosting' center of trade and manufacture, the commercial metropolis of the eastern Mediterranean. She had her Academies and Lyceums, but she had also her Rotary Clubs; at the foot of the Acropolis, crowned with the temples of the gods, lay the noisy, crowded, ill-smelling retail market; not far away were the thronging wholesale districts and dockyards of the Piræus, and the grim industrial district round about Laurium, where the air was polluted by the noisome fumes from innumerable smelters.

Fortunately for the generations of

men to come, not all, or even much, of Athens was like this. Perhaps the less pleasing portions of the picture have been allowed to thrust themselves too much into the foreground. But I would have you keep always in mind that not every Athenian spent his days in singing hymns to the Olympian gods, or debating ultimate metaphysics; in listening to great masterpieces of tragedy, or impressing a fleeting glimpse of beauty upon Pentelic marble. Many were busied with the more banal tasks of trade and manufacture and finance. This less fortunate and less famous portion of the population cannot be left out in estimating the debt we owe to Greece, or in seeking to trace the long process that has given the modern business man an adequate apparatus and fairly advanced standards of honesty and service.

Having, I trust, succeeded in bringing the ancient Athenian to life, we may now listen to his defense against the imputation of unmitigated rascality. In the quality of his advocate, I will begin by admitting, cheerfully, that there were rascals of every description in this pagan metropolis, for Greeks, when they did set out to be rascals, yielded to none. And before we proceed with the more serious part of our inquiry, I wish to spend a little time, for my own delectation and yours, in chatting about Athenian swindlers — many of them rascals whom I have come to love for their very rascality.

Let me present first a pair of knaves, named Hegestratus and Xenothemis, specialists in the art of swindling the men who financed shipping ventures. On one occasion, finding themselves in Syracuse, on a ship commanded by Hegestratus, they negotiated heavy loans by the simple device of presenting as security a cargo which belonged to others. The money, as it came into their hands, was remitted to their home town, Marseilles, and they undertook to cover up the fraud by sinking the ship at sea, since the loss of a cargo in shipping loans fell upon the lender and not the borrower. Unfortunately for the success of their plans, Hegestratus was clumsy in his attempt to scuttle the

An old case

ship, and made so much noise that he was discovered; he jumped overboard to escape the enraged passengers, missed the boat in which he and his confederate were to have escaped, and was drowned. Xenothemis pretended to be as much surprised and appalled at his villainy as any one, and had the effrontery, when the ship reached Athens, to claim ownership of her cargo. Swindlers who practiced this and other kinds of fraud for which the terms of bottomry contracts left an opening were to be found in every Greek port, and those who made the Piræus their headquarters were actually organized into associations.

The splendid opportunities afforded by the visits to town of the rural population were not overlooked even in these early times, and it is likely that the Parthenon was sold at least as often as the Flatiron Building. The perils to which the country gentleman was exposed in the city are well illustrated by the way in which Athenogenes and a beautiful woman accomplice, Antigone, victimized a wealthy young rustic. The latter wished to purchase a slave from Athenogenes, and was persuaded to sign an agreement in which he assumed responsibility for whatever obligations the man might have contracted. Athenogenes assured him verbally that these were trifling bits of indebtedness, incurred by the slave in the daily routine of business, and included in the transaction merely as a matter of convenience. The victim signed on the dotted line, and within a short time after the purchase learned he had made himself legally liable for amounts that totaled a good-sized fortune.

If we should set ourselves to the task, we should be able to find many sorts of rascality—all of them, unfortunately, still familiar in these enlightened days —and to add to our collection many fascinating sketches of gentlemen who lived by their wits. But the topic which began as a playful digression cannot be allowed to monopolize our attention; we must be content with a judicious selection. Unquestionably the place of honor goes to the 'shyster' lawyer; in spite of stringent legal enactments intended to discourage his existence, he was almost as numerous and quite as enterprising in Athens as in our own large cities; an entire book and a very interesting one has been devoted to him lately by an American scholar. Like his modern descendant, his multifarious activities ranged all the way from flagrant blackmail and wholesale bribery to petty bits of chicanery, which he would execute at an extremely modest rate of compensation; he was always ready to forge or falsify a legal instrument, for the customary fee, and could usually furnish witnesses in batches of any desired number at so much per head. There is the dishonest trustee, who defrauded the widow and the orphan, whose victims were only too often his own near relations and friends. Nor must we forget the embezzlers or the bank wreckers, who found a rich field for their talents in Athens, but occasionally thought it advisable to travel abroad for the good of their health. Or, if you are weary of such small fry, and would hear of the 'predatory interests,' who operated on a grander scale, we may turn to allegations that certain individuals and companies made colossal profits by the manipulation of mining concessions or by 'grabbing' mineral lands belonging to the state. Here, however, it must be said in fairness, we are dealing with accusations upon which the state not infrequently

refused to take legal action, for fear
of 'discouraging legitimate enterprise.'
Yet the fact that such charges were
seriously advanced in the courts shows
that peculation on a large scale was not
unknown. There were also individuals,
you will regret to hear, so lost to every
sense of decency that they would actually attempt to corner the wheat market in order to make a 'killing.' Such
commercial depravity as this, I make
haste to add, in Athens was punished
with death. Finally we must not pass
by the typical 'deadbeat.' He may not
deserve a place with real artists in the
swindlers' hall of fame, but without his
portrait the collection would be in-
complete. You will be grieved to learn

that the most notorious deadbeat of ancient Athens, Æschines by name, was one of the pupils of Socrates. The merchants in the Piræus vowed there was less risk in a venture to the stormy Adriatic than in a loan to Æschines, for when he had once got a loan he hung on to it more tenaciously than an inheritance; the shops in his locality were often closed, because the proprietors were all in court suing him for unpaid accounts; his neighbors vacated the homes they owned, and rented in other parts of the city to avoid his 'touches'; the crowds of bill collectors thronging to his house at daybreak made passers-by think some one was dead and a funeral going on. However, Æschines ended his days in prosperity; he married an old lady who was no beauty, to be sure, for she had more fingers than teeth, but brought him an immense fortune. This quaint description may be a calumny upon Æschines — for Socrates' sake we trust it is — but it shows the antiquity of a type which our retail credit associations have not yet been able to eradicate completely.

Having listened to this, you cannot suspect me of suppressing the truth or glossing over what is discreditable in the attempt to portray the Athenians as more honest than they were; in fact, if I have anywhere failed in fidelity to my sources, I have yielded to a natural human instinct to touch up the picture, rather than to tone it down. Yet I would ask you to remember that this material is taken chiefly from the arguments of litigants or counsel before a court, and by its very nature exhibits the seamy side of life. References in court to an opposing litigant seldom dwell upon his more attractive qualities, and even anecdotes introduced by way of illustration are apt to be exaggerated for the sake of a point. In any fairly decent community, transactions which find their way into the courts represent the exception rather than the rule, and a record of litigation cannot be taken as an index of general moral standards. However, let us grant for the sake of argument that all the stories of rascality are literally true. They still do not justify the inference that a majority of Athenians were unprincipled, or the general tone of morality in their business relations low. They prove exactly what I have already so willingly admitted, that Greeks, when they were rascals, were intelligent and effective rascals; if they chose dishonesty as a career, they brought to it the joyous energy and intellectual acumen that made them successful in other more creditable activities. Again we must remember we are dealing with a community of human beings. In any such community there will be some who are far below the general standards of honor and morality and some as far above it, while the great mass of the population will be distributed between the two extremes. Our inquiry is not primarily concerned with the exceptions; we are seeking rather to determine what was the general level of morality in business, in practice as well as in abstract doctrine. If this is to be done, we must have all the data available, and must strike our balance only when both sides of the account have been subjected to equally careful scrutiny. Moreover, since we have undertaken to determine what contribution, if any, the Greeks made to the elevation of business standards, we cannot be content with an examination of the principles and practices they handed down to their successors. It will be necessary to consider what Greece learned from her oriental neighbors in the times of her apprenticeship, and we shall have to go back to the earlier stages of her history.

II

THANKS to the archæological discoveries which came so thick and fast toward the close of the last century, we have now considerable information relating to commerce and industry in the eastern Mediterranean before the coming of the Greeks. Fifty years ago the existence of the Minoan Empire was unknown; to-day we can trace the gradual development of its industries back through the centuries to the rude culture of the late Stone Age, and follow its principal trade routes from Asia Minor and Egypt far into the

unknown and barbarous regions of the
west. Unfortunately, since the record is
archæological — for the writing of this
people has not yet been deciphered — we
know practically nothing regarding the
commercial law and custom of the Minoans, their standards of morality in business, or the personalities of their captains
of industry. The material wealth and
grandeur they attained, however, and
the vast proportions of their trade cannot be doubted. For many centuries
their commercial intercourse with Egypt
and the East went on without interrup-
tion, and we shall probably be not far
from the truth if we conclude that their
economic and social institutions, as well
as their commercial law and morality,

were similar to those of the Nile and Euphrates valleys, with which we are better acquainted. In certain departments of art and industry — in the manufacture of pottery, in the working of metals, the engraving of precious stones, in mural decoration, and in matters of sanitation — the Minoans had equaled or outstripped the achievements of any other people. We begin to see undeniable evidence that the craftsman has a conscious pride in the fineness and beauty of his work, and this is perhaps a step toward a realization of the fact that industry and trade exist, not for profit alone, but also for the service of society; it is the first flickering gleam of the professional spirit.

The subversion of this culture consequent upon the gradual infiltration of
the Hellenes probably began as early as
the eighteenth century before Christ.
By the twelfth or eleventh century it
was complete, and the brilliant civilization we have sketched had been replaced
by a distinctly primitive condition of
society. Minoan commerce had been
swept from the seas, the wealth of its
great cities was destroyed or dissipated,
and what little survived of its art and
industry had undergone marked deteri-
oration. At the beginning of the first
millennium before Christ the mode of
life described in the Homeric poems
prevailed throughout the islands and
shores of the Ægean. The territory once

dominated by the kings of Cnossus was
now occupied by a large number of in-
significant tribal monarchies, not unlike
the primitive Celtic clans. Within these
groups political and economic arrangements were extremely simple and infor-
mal. The Homeric king, unlike the
semi-divine potentate of Egypt and
Mesopotamia, was not the owner of
the tribal lands, but only of a royal
demesne of moderate extent; the great
bulk of the territory occupied by the
group was allotted to the patriarchal
families for fields and vineyards or used
in common for pasture lands. Reli-
gious endowments were on an equally
modest scale, and only a comparatively
small part of the tribal domain was

comprised in the sacred precincts attached to the unpretentious shrines of the gods. In marked contrast to the oriental empires, with their extortionate taxes and tithes for church and throne, the expenses of government and religion were slight. The folk assembled for war bringing their own equipment and provision, and when they gathered for a common sacrifice each family provided its quota of victims. Taxation was unnecessary in such a simple form of organization and therefore practically unknown.

Although title to real property was vested in the family, or perhaps even in the tribal group, personal property belonged to individuals. The prevailing economy was that of the patriarchal household, which produced independently the food, clothing, arms, and simple agricultural equipment needed by its members. Although the faint beginnings of specialization in manufacture may be traced, especially in those arts which require a maximum of skill, yet the tasks of smith and carpenter and wheelwright were usually performed by the head of the family, with the assistance of his sons and servants. The pursuits of peace, mainly agriculture and stock raising, were limited to what was sufficient to provide the necessities of life. Extremes of wealth and poverty were probably rare, since there was little opportunity for piling up great fortunes, and every member of society had a claim to maintenance from the resources of the community. Under these circumstances, such trade as took place between different communities was of the most elementary description; coined money was unknown, the unit of value in the estimation of wealth was the worth of an ox, and exchange took the form of a barter of commodities in kind. How slight and primitive was this inter-tribal commerce of the Homeric Greeks we gather from the poet Hesiod's description of a typical trading voyage in his time, several centuries later. When the harvest was over and the annual yield stored and checked against the probable needs of the ensuing winter, the head of the household would gather his surplus together, load it into the fragile boat his own hands had built, and coast cautiously along neighboring shores, bartering his goods for the excess commodities of others. Such commerce as this afforded but slight opportunity for the acquisition of wealth, and we are not surprised to learn from the Homeric poems that war, and not trade, was the favorite mode of increasing one's possessions. The man of strength and prowess, who headed a powerful family group, was not only the political and social leader of his community, but the man of wealth; piracy and cattle lifting were recognized and reputable occupations in this heroic age.

There was, however, another type of trade than the simple barter of commodities between neighboring communities. The Homeric Greeks are known to have possessed articles, such as ivory and amber, which came from distant lands; and this seems to point to trade relations more regular and extensive than those we have just discussed. Furthermore there are allusions to professional merchants and traders, ranging all the way from the man who commands his own ship and crew to the humble peddler who travels from port to port with a little stock of goods, taking passage on whatever vessel may chance to come his way. These professional traders were the Phœnicians, who seized upon the opportunity presented by the decline of Egyptian and Minoan commerce, and were for many centuries the common carriers of the Mediterranean world. Now the Phœnicians, I regret to say, had a very poor reputation for honesty and fair dealing, and for this there were several reasons. To begin with, they followed no regular routes, but traveled hither and thither almost at random, trading first with one community and then with another as opportunity offered. Consequently they established no permanent connections, and were not under any necessity of practicing that fair dealing which looks to a cultivation of future trade; knowing that the whole Mediterranean lay open to them and they need never see their victims again, they doubtless cheated at every opportunity, and invariably drove as hard a bargain as they could. Again, they were trading with a people which stood upon a much lower cultural level than their own, and they looked upon the Hellenic tribesmen as fit and proper subjects for unscrupulous exploitation — an attitude which unfortunately still characterizes some modern nations in their commercial intercourse with more backward peoples. Finally, since the Greeks produced little if anything that had an export value, aside from the numerous captives taken in their incessant wars and piratical forays, their commerce with the Phœnicians must have been principally in slaves, and the slave trade notoriously in all times and places makes for low standards of morality. This will explain why the Homeric Greeks regarded the professional merchant with distrust and contempt, and how the Phœnicians got their evil reputation as kidnapers.

Trade, having its beginning under such conditions as these, was naturally looked upon by the Greeks for many centuries as an occupation unworthy of a freeman and a gentleman, and only very gradually in the course of time did it improve its status and its standards of morality and fair dealing. Since the men of the Homeric age regarded war and piracy as the natural method of acquiring wealth, their earliest commercial intercourse was founded upon mutual distrust and the desire to outwit an opponent, and not upon considerations of reciprocal advantage and satisfaction. And this primitive point of view was confirmed by their dealings with the Phœnicians, who looked upon them merely as possible victims of exploitation and sharp practice, and taught them little or nothing of what the oriental world then possessed in the way of commercial law or morality. Yet, after a comparatively short lapse of time—five or six centuries at the most—Hellas had made her trade and industry the economic basis for a higher and finer type of culture than the world had ever known, and the activities of business and finance stood almost as high in the social scale as they do to-day. The process by which this came about is an interesting one, and well worth study.

The political history of the Greeks from beginning to end illustrates most impressively the intimate relation between the economic condition of a people and its political practices. The primitive tribal monarchy of Homeric times was the inevitable product of long centuries of war and migration in which there was constant need of centralized leadership. It was not so well adapted to the conditions which followed the occupation and conquest of the Ægean area, and the operation of economic and

social forces engendered by a more settled agricultural life gradually trans-
formed it into aristocracy. This type of
government in turn was unable to main-
tain itself in those communities in which
the rapid growth of trade and industry
had shifted the balance of economic
power. When it broke down, the limited
political experience of the Hellenes,
and the presence in almost every state
of factions with differing interests and
purposes, made it impossible to devise
quickly and peacefully new institutions
to meet their new problems. Consequently the period of industrial and
commercial expansion was at first a period of political and social unrest, of un-
certainty and experimentation in state-

craft, so frequently marked by monarchic reaction that it has been called the Age of the Tyrants. By the fifth century, those states which were not subjected to external pressure had worked out schemes of political organization suited to their needs.

In very early times, down to the eighth century or thereabouts, the various forces which brought about economic and political change seem to have operated quite generally and uniformly over the entire Ægean area, and the result is a cultural unity which makes the task of the historian comparatively simple. But with the breakdown of the aristocracies and the sudden expansion of trade and manufacture, divergency becomes the rule; from this point on, the economic history of the Greeks must be broken up into a number of distinct chapters, and a collective treatment is no longer possible. In some states agriculture continued to be the economic basis of life, and changes of a social or political character were introduced only very gradually; in others an advantageous situation with respect to trade routes brought about a rapid growth of commerce and consequent alteration in the social fabric; still others, finding themselves in possession of valuable raw materials, embarked upon manufacture; many states which were embarrassed by the poverty of their soil and the demands of increasing population found in industrial or commercial activities a way of self-preservation.

Amid the diversity of this period, we find one element of unity which has to do with the very essence of our inquiry. In the process of commercial expansion and colonization those of the Greek people who had abandoned agriculture for trade or industry were brought more and more into relations with the peoples of Asia Minor. This contact was very different from the sporadic intercourse of an earlier age with such free-lances of commerce as the Phœnicians. Now for the first time the Greeks had an opportunity to study the methods and standards which had been evolved in the course of long ages by their eastern neighbors. They studied them to good effect, and it is no exaggeration to say that the body of mercantile law and usage which they had developed by the fourth century before Christ had as its nucleus the practices and legal rules of the east. Not all Greeks, of course, were subjected to these influences equally early or in the same measure, but the general result was a body of common law having to do with mercantile transactions that ultimately was recognized everywhere throughout the Mediterranean, and later went to the making of the Roman law.

Miletus, Mytilene, Ægina, Corinth, Megara, Chalcis—these are but a few of many Greek cities which speedily became centers of industry and trade. Each of them has its history, which it would be fascinating to reconstruct bit by bit from the hints of ancient writers and from the more concrete evidence that is constantly being brought to light by archæological research. We may, however, limit our attention for the present to Athens, since it is Athens which eventually became, for a brief and brilliant time, the commercial, political, and intellectual leader of the eastern Mediterranean.

Athens was more or less influenced toward the substitution of commercial and industrial pursuits for agriculture by all three of the causes that have been enumerated. Her harbors were conveniently accessible to merchants following the east and west trade route across the Isthmus of Corinth. Her deposits of excellent potter's clay favored the early establishment and steady growth of the ceramic industry for which Attica was famous, and, as time went on, other mineral resources, notably the rich deposits of silver-lead ore at Laurium, contributed to her industrial expansion. With the increase in wealth and population consequent upon commercial development, the poverty of her soil became more and more apparent, and by the fifth century it was obvious that her fortune lay along the lines of commercial and industrial enterprise rather than agriculture.

The social and political changes engendered by these economic factors followed the general course already sketched. The old aristocratic régime that had flourished when agriculture was the economic foundation of society gave way, reluctantly and after grim civil strife, before the attacks of the lower orders. The famous tyrant Pisistratus established a monarchy, and for more than fifty years he and his sons were rulers of the state. Under their sway commerce and industry flourished as never before, and Athens laid the foundations of the great economic strength that was to be hers in days to come. Upon the expulsion of the tyrants, the mercantile and laboring classes insisted upon a political status commensurate with their economic importance, and the early part of the fifth century saw Athens well embarked upon the course which was to end in the first democracy the world had ever seen.

Prejudice and tradition, we must remember, die hard, and even in the age of Pericles, while the Athenians were enjoying the pleasure and power that came to them from their extensive trade, their rich silver mines, their industries of one sort and another, they still clung tenaciously to the old feeling that agriculture was the only gainful occupation befitting a free man and a citizen. It was not until agriculture had finally received its death blow in the

Peloponnesian War that this feeling disappeared, and the capitalist, the merchant, and the manufacturer came to be thought of as really respectable members of society.

At the beginning of the fourth century, the Athenians faced the difficult task of recovering in some measure the wealth that had been destroyed or dissipated during years of incessant warfare. Not only were they confronted with an empty treasury, but most private fortunes had dwindled or totally disappeared. In some respects their situation was not unlike that of the Southern States in the lean years of reconstruction. Fortunately the Athenians were wise enough to realize that they could not look to agriculture to recuperate their shattered fortunes, but must exploit to the full the possibilities of trade and manufacture. What was left of their agricultural resources was not neglected; the old aristocratic predilection for country life was still sufficiently strong in most cases to draw back the owners of the land to their wasted fields and vineyards. But even the capital needed to restore the ravages of war had often to be sought in the realm of trade, and many families once wealthy were compelled to toil for the bare necessities of life. Men whose sole task had been the direction of their slaves went into business or even worked for hire, and gentlewomen learned to follow for profit

the occupations that once had beguiled
their leisure hours.

With the slow return of prosperity,
the lessons learnt in the school of ad-
versity were not forgotten. Country life
and farming were still grateful to the
Athenian spirit, and few Athenians ever
lost completely their dislike of manual
labor or their contempt for retail trade
on a small scale. But the economic basis
of society and the state in the fourth
century was trade and industry, and the
fact was frankly recognized in the social
and political arrangements of the time.
Simple and frugal as were Greek standards of living, a city of perhaps two
hundred thousand souls needed urgently
every penny of capital that could be

put to productive use. The men who could create capital or command it were now the men who shouldered the burdens of society; success in business came to mean social advancement, citizenship, and political preferment. Even the law felt the influence of this changed attitude, and special courts with speedy forms of action were established to give the capitalist the encouragement of security. It is in Athens in the fourth century that Greek trade and industry first attain their full development, and it is here we must seek if we would learn what the Greeks have contributed in the way of moral standards to the law and custom they received from their eastern neighbors.

III

FROM what has been said you will perhaps understand that the Athenians of the fourth century lived in an environment not altogether unlike our own. After the brilliant outburst of creative genius and the intellectual activity of the fifth century, they had quietly settled down to be a prosperous commercial and industrial community. The man in the street no doubt regarded the intellectual achievements of his generation with some complacency, and felt that the human race had comparatively little more to learn. Also he was becoming increasingly aware of his material needs, and of the various comforts and conveniences which could be bought with money. The creative genius of the Greek race, in so far as it was still at work, was now directed mainly to the creation of capital. The forces of commerce and industry had been increased, perhaps by defections from the ranks of art and literature, philosophy and science, and Athens was experiencing the smug satisfaction in the joys of material well-being that occasionally to-day finds expression in a hymn of praise. It would be quite misleading, however, to stress too greatly the elements of similarity. The differences are far more striking, and it is of the utmost importance that we keep these differences constantly in mind. To begin with, the Athenian's standard of living would impress the modern observer as actually meager. His physical wants were surprisingly few and easily satisfied. What contented the most luxurious in the matter of clothing, food, and shelter, would now be deemed insufficient, if not actually disgraceful, for those in very moderate circumstances. Yet the Athenian had the advantage of us in at least one respect; he was not under the necessity of devoting his whole time and thought to the acquisition of physical necessities. He could and did in many ways take life more easily and more calmly than we to-day. He had more time than we for the demands of state and of religion. He had more time for keeping physically fit, and for enjoyment, and, finally, much more time for thought. Although business had become respectable and its rewards desirable, it was still but a means toward an end, and that end one of many of which the Athenian remained constantly aware. The most able and energetic merchant of those times would probably look upon the hurry and hustle of a modern American city as something essentially barbarous, and the life of the average American business man would seem to him better suited for a slave. He might even venture to remind us, courteously, that civilization is after all a process of fitting the individual into a gregarious scheme of existence, and one may have all the material conveniences of which we are so proud and still be essentially uncivilized. In other words, the Greek brought to his business life the frugal habit, the good taste, the restraint, the happy faculty of striking the mean, that governed his activities in other fields. This temperament obviously should find its expression in sound standards of morality in trade.

It must, of course, be fairly evident that what we have in mind is a great deal more than merely common honesty. We must recur to the definition with which we started, and ask whether the Hellenes had come to realize that the proper function of business is not the blind production and acquisition of wealth, but the improvement of human life, and whether they had succeeded to an appreciable extent in directing the actual operations of business toward the adequate performance of this function. We shall wish first to consider briefly the economic theories of the philosophers, and then to examine the conditions which actually prevailed in the business world, as reflected in political and social organization, in civil legislation, and in the custom and usage that governed the operations of trade and finance. If our inquiry is to keep its liaison with the known facts of history, and not to wander off into abstract speculation, we shall be quite as much concerned with standards of individual honesty as with the collective sense of responsibility to society.

For untold ages men have been stringing together proverbial bits of practical wisdom and morality, many of them applicable to economic problems. This elementary stage of economic thought has not been, and probably never will be, left entirely behind us. We can easily follow its tradition from the *Farmer's Almanac* composed by the poet Hesiod in the eighth century before Christ, through the elegies of Theognis and Isocrates' *Advice to a Young Man*, down to Poor Richard, our twentieth-century literature of success, and the *Vim, Vigor, Victory Verses* of Mr. Herbert Kaufman. It was apparently in the Socratic and other contemporary schools of philosophy, so far as we can judge from our fragmentary sources, that such inchoate masses of empirical thought first came into the environment which was eventually to mold them into a science. In the fifth and fourth centuries the data of economics were being studied systematically and its fundamental concepts subjected to critical analysis; now for the first time apparently general principles were formulated in a conscious attempt to correlate and explain the facts of economic life and to establish norms for the better performance of economic functions. Thus economics is one of those disciplines that owe their beginning to the peculiar temper of the

Greek mind, with its passion for discovery constantly controlled and directed by a fondness for orderly and accurate thinking.

I shall make no attempt to present even briefly the history of Greek economic thought. This has been discussed repeatedly and with much detail by competent specialists, and a valuable monograph on the subject has been published by an American scholar within the last ten years. We are concerned here with the general approach of the Greek philosophers to the ethical side of economics, and with the probable effects of their teaching upon the standards of morality which prevailed in the world of trade. Allowance must necessarily be made for the great difference between the simple environment in which the study of these problems was first undertaken and the vast complexity of our modern economic life. We must be prepared to find the limitations, errors, and confusions inseparable from the elementary stages of any discipline. Nor should we emphasize too much the failure of the Greeks in some instances to answer correctly the difficult questions with which they found themselves confronted; what is really remarkable is that these questions should have been asked at all, in this early time. Yet many of the principles formulated in the fifth and fourth centuries are still fundamental postulates of economics, and some of the queries to which the answers could not then be found are still unanswered.

In general the limitations of the Greek economists are least serious in the field of our inquiry. The reproach most frequently brought against them, that they did not define precisely the field of economics, but confused it on the one side with ethics and on the other with politics, is in itself sufficient evidence that they were chiefly interested in the moral and social aspects of the science, rather than in problems of material organization. Furthermore, the changes which have come with increasing complexity of economic environment have affected social and moral issues in less degree than they have questions which relate to organization and methods. The balance sheet of a great modern corporation, when contrasted with the simple accounts of an ancient merchant, will look like the formulas of the theory of relativity set over against a sum in simple arithmetic. But the question whether it is honest, and for the best interest of society, to corner the market in some staple necessity, and then disseminate false reports regarding sources of supply, is to-day essentially what it was in the time of Lysias. The technique of salesmanship has changed enormously, the moral problems very little indeed; our formulas of efficiency are quite unlike those of the ancient world, but the fundamental principles of honesty remain the same.

We may not agree with Xenophon in believing it expedient that the state should enter into competition with private enterprise in trade, but we readily see that his proposals for public ownership were intended to improve the standard of living of the poorer citizens. Plato's schemes for stringent regulation of trade and finance may not impress us as wholly wise, yet obviously they have this same intent. Again, there is Aristotle's distinction between the false and the true arts of acquisition, of which the one makes money an end in itself and aims at unlimited riches, while the

IA

other has as its goal the promotion of well being by the production and proper use of wealth. Although we cannot in many instances assent to his specific classification of trades, the general principle of his distinction is precisely that from which our discussion took its start. Whichever way we may look, we shall find abundant evidence that Greek economic theory was founded upon the humanitarian principles which underlie the thought of many economists to-day.

Here you may ask what effect the abstract speculations of the Academy or Lyceum could have had upon actual standards of morality in trade. You may remind me, pertinently enough, that the modern business man seldom goes to the moral philosopher for guidance, or even hears the voice that is gently raised in academic expostulation. But the case was different in Athens. The criticism of the Socratic school represented the opinion, not merely of a few harmless idealists, but also of a conservative element still strong enough economically and politically to make its influence distinctly felt. Nowhere are the old prejudice against the bourgeoisie and the aristocratic predilection for country life more apparent than in the writings of the philosophers. The Athenian captain of industry was subjected to a criticism that was measurably hostile, and therefore the more searching, and also measurably powerful, as emanating from the upper levels of society; it could not easily be brushed aside as empty theory or stigmatized as 'Bolshevistic.' On the other side was the sovereign people, calling for 'service.' Between the devil and the deep sea, the Athenian man of business had of necessity to give some thought to his responsibilities.

With these last considerations, we have entered upon the political and social aspects of our problem. Here our task is to study trade and industry in their relation to the state, and here we shall discover, in my opinion, the greatest contribution ancient Greece has made to economic progress. That the Hellenes first introduced into the world the ideal of constitutional government and political freedom of the individual, is a commonplace. Yet most of us fail to realize, what is equally true, that they also developed and applied, for the first time in history, the principles of economic freedom. Since this is to give them credit for what is probably the most important single step in the whole course of economic evolution, the grounds upon which I make the assertion must be stated briefly.

Although the Hellenes learned much from their eastern neighbors, especially in matters of industrial organization, technical processes, and methods of exchange, their economic system was essentially unlike anything that had developed in the East. It was to all intents and purposes a new creation, differing from the oriental system as fundamentally as the little city-state differed from the vast tax-gathering empire. We cannot now undertake to determine all the various forces which combined to bring about these two divergent lines of economic development, but may profitably turn our attention to two factors of especial importance, the underlying theories of government and the prevailing conditions of land tenure. Turning first to the East, we see that the history of government is the story of a process of aggregation into larger and larger units. This process began, both in Egypt and in the valley of the Euphrates, with tiny agricultural communities, which were gradually welded together, first into city-states, then into kingdoms, and finally into colossal tax-gathering empires. Just as the despotic powers of the semi-divine potentates who ruled over these territories in historic times go back to the prerogatives of the priest-kings who governed the primitive city-states, so the origin of the oriental economic system is to be sought in early conditions and theories of land tenure. In the beginning, the land was thought of, not as the property of individuals or families, or even of communities, but as belonging to the gods, and later to the priest-kings, their representatives. The folk who tilled the soil, being merely tenants and not owners, paid heavy rentals in the form of tithes to temple and to palace. Hence individual ownership of land and the notion of private property developed slowly and imperfectly. For example, in Egypt, even under the later Pharaohs, only a slight proportion of the arable land was at any time really the property of individuals; in other countries, where private ownership was more fully developed, the lingering effects of the ancient theories are plainly seen in the inordinate taxation which harassed the operations of trade and restricted industrial expansion. Everywhere throughout these kingdoms and empires political tyranny went hand in hand with merciless economic exploitation of the land and of the people. Here we have an impressive argument for the view that consumption, not production, may be the central problem of economics. Although these ancient nations made great progress in the arts of production, the wealth that might have gone to adequate development of natural resources and improvement in the general standard of living was dissipated in ways that were mainly unproductive. The treasures wrung from a toiling population went to satisfy the whims of an irresponsible despot or the demands of an insatiate priesthood, to the erection of costly palaces and tombs, the maintenance of luxurious courts, of huge armies, of parasitic hordes of public functionaries. In such a system of exploitation, corruption ran rife, and official dishonesty added its quota to the burdens under which the peasants groaned. If you feel that this is exaggerated, you have but to turn to the actual records, and read King Urukagina's account of the oppression and abuse that were rampant in the ancient kingdom of Lagash when he came to the throne, or note what Harmhab, a Pharaoh of sense and sympathy, tells us of conditions in Egypt in the fourteenth century B.C. Or we may remember that at one time practically all of the arable land in Egypt not included in the royal domains belonged to the temples, and one person in every fifty of the population was a temple slave. Incalculable labor that might have made possible a decent standard of living went to provide the colossal gold and silver ornaments of the temples. The mortuary service at a prince's tomb absorbed the income from twelve towns in perpetuity, and we are told the labor of one hundred thousand men over a period of twenty years was required for the erection of Khufu's last resting place. The golden treasures from the tomb of Tutenkhamon on which we feast our eyes have cost the life blood of untold thousands.

Simple and poor as was the life of the average Greek beside our luxurious existence, it was nothing short of magnificent in comparison with what the common folk of other races knew. The poverty of Greece was that noble poverty which Montesquieu has termed a part of their liberty.* In the little tribal groups from which the Hellenic city-state evolved, the warrior king had but a fair domain, proportionate to the services he rendered; and the plots of ground attached to the shrines of the gods were as modest as the simple temples they surrounded. As has been said, the greater part of the land was divided among the patriarchal families for fields and vineyards, or used in common as pasturage for flocks. And when in the

* *De l'Esprit des Lois,* xx. 3; quoted by Zimmern, *The Greek Commonwealth* (4 ed., 1924), 213.

course of time individual ownership
developed, it was ownership with no
lingering trace of tenancy, loaded with
no duties to a feudal lord. Here and
there, mainly in Dorian states, a con-
quered pre-Dorian population lived on
as serfs, but in general a large proportion
of the population were landowners. So
strong was the sense of the individual's
right in property that a tax on land was
unusual in the Greek democracies. The
economic freedom that had its beginning in the age of agriculture endured
to determine the course of commercial
development, and the tasks of industry
and trade were committed to the private
enterprise of freemen. The wealth thus
produced went in greater measure than

ever before to improve the general standard of living. Demands of religion were met liberally, though never profusely. The state practiced the same simple frugality that characterized the life of the individual. In many ways the public finance of the Greeks appears to us childish and improvident, but the fact remains that their governments generally found it possible to meet their obligations, even through long periods of incessant warfare, without increasing taxation to a point where it became oppressive.

Collectively and individually, theoretically and in practice, the Greeks acknowledged the responsibilities that attach to the possession of wealth. No-

thing could be more offensive to a normal Greek than cant regarding the
'sacredness' of private property, or the
notion that wealth is to be used as the
possessor may please, without regard to
the interests of humanity or social conse-
quences. The state had always the right
to require from her citizens and residents
financial support proportionate to their
means, just as she might call for their
personal service as soldiers, or sailors,
or public functionaries. Sometimes, as I
have hinted, the demands of a democracy
upon its wealthy class tended to become
exacting. Yet, with all this, the Athenians of the fourth century enjoyed as a
heritage from their forefathers such economic freedom as the world had never

dreamt of. Industry, from the wretched slave of despots, had become the valued servant of society.

Here someone is sure to remind me that this economic freedom and these more tolerable conditions of daily life, among the Greeks, did not affect the total population, and Hellenic culture was founded upon slavery. But this is, after all, perhaps only another way of saying that the Greeks have not yet solved the vast and intricate problems associated with the widely divergent capacities of individuals and races for industrial and social usefulness. To modern society, with its world-wide inter-relations, these problems are nearer and more serious than to the little city-state

—and they are not yet solved. We can no longer pretend there is a definite and distinct line of demarcation between slavery and freedom, and a man is free if only he cannot be bought and sold as a chattel. Slavery and freedom, like health and disease, shade into one another by insensible gradations. Which of the so-called superior races to-day is ready to give complete freedom—social, political, economic—to the members of an inferior race with which it must live and perhaps compete? Who will affirm that the nominal freemen who are hewers of wood and drawers of water in the world to-day are, all of them, everywhere, more truly free than the Athenian slave? Many of them certainly have fewer material comforts, and perhaps less happiness. It is not my intention to defend slavery, but merely to point out that the Greeks were dealing with a problem which is not yet solved and cannot be solved merely by proclamations of emancipation. What progress they had made, however, becomes apparent when we reflect that they had extended the blessings of freedom and the ordinary comforts of life to classes which could never have hoped for them under the older economic order. They had replaced a society in which all but a very few were slaves by one in which many were free.

Unfortunately such conditions as these were not destined to endure. With the loss of Greek freedom, a period of retrogression began. The Hellenistic princes modeled the economic organization of their kingdoms, not upon the Greek commonwealth, but upon the oriental tax-gathering empire; and the Roman emperors introduced throughout the civilized world the pernicious type of state finance that the Ptolemies had inherited from the ancient Pharaohs. The economic system with which Europe emerged from the Middle Ages was in great part, like her political and legal institutions and her social order, a hotch-potch of fag ends from oriental despotism, feudalism, and monarchy founded on divine right.

The commercial law which developed

in the Greek atmosphere of political and economic freedom embodied an advanced conception of civil justice. It had the simple, clear, orderly character we have learned to look for in the various expressions of the Greek temperament and character. The complicated legal questions that arise in the relationships of business were dealt with more effectively than might be expected from the comparative simplicity of economic life and business organization. Nor was the commercial law of Athens an isolated development, unrelated to that of the city-states which surrounded her on every side. It was part of a great body of common law regulating commercial intercourse; its fundamental principles were recognized throughout the Hellenic world and could be enforced in the courts of many cities. The special legal problems that arise in connection with particular industries and particular forms of commercial enterprise were given due attention. Thus Athens had its banking law, its shipping law, and its law of mines, enforced by courts of special civil jurisdiction through special forms of action.

The general characteristics of the Attic law are now more widely known than was the case a few years ago. It looked to intent rather than form. It aimed at as great expedition in the administration of justice as was consistent with a scrupulous regard for the legal rights of individuals, and it betrayed a distinct tendency to favor considerations of equity as opposed to strict interpretations of the law. It endeavored to minimize the disadvantages to which the poor man is inevitably exposed when he seeks justice through the courts by providing speedy, inexpensive forms of trial before public arbitrators.

Although the Greeks received from their eastern neighbors many of the fundamental principles of their commercial law, one need only contrast the Attic law of the fourth century with Babylonian law to see that here, as in other fields, the Greeks have made a very real advance; for Babylonian law, surprising as it is for its place and time,

is after all a very primitive and elementary system when compared with
the Greek. Although it dealt not in-
effectively with the problem of justice
as between individuals, we cannot but
observe that it is the justice imposed
by a master upon his slaves, and not
the justice administered between free
citizens by tribunals of their peers.

In this perhaps more than any other
field what the Greeks achieved was continued and preserved under the Hellenistic kings and later the Roman emperors. The Hellenistic rulers, despite their
autocratic power, made little attempt
to interfere with the private rights of
Greeks settled in their realms, and the
civil law of the Greek commonwealths

survived in the *nomos politikos* of the
Hellenistic colonies. It had lost some
of the spirit, but kept much of the form
and many of the fundamental principles
of the classic Greek law. Meanwhile,
in Rome the prætors and jurisconsults,
in substituting for the primitive formal-
istic law of early republican times a
workable system adequate to the commercial activities of an empire, drew
largely upon the Hellenic common law
that still governed the operations of trade
in the Mediterranean world. Under the
emperors there lingered a tradition of
the old freedom and equality which once
had been the pride of Roman citizens,
and the private law of the Roman empire
never, even in the darkest times of im-

perial tyranny or prætorian anarchy, lost completely the character it owed in some measure to the Greeks.

It is not difficult, when the political and legal institutions of a community are known in general outline, to make comparisons and form credible conclusions in regard to prevailing standards of conduct. The questions which have to do with the personalities of individuals, their characters and ideals and actions, are not so easy to answer. Yet even here materials are not wholly lacking if we seek with care. For example, we get a pretty good notion of Athenian standards of propriety and conduct toward the close of the fourth century from the *Characters* of Theophrastus.

For it is obvious that the society which laughed at his pictures of the Long-Winded Man, the Good Fellow, the Fourflusher, the Knocker, the Grumbler, the Roughneck, expected of a gentleman, in the ordinary relations of life, a decent reserve, modesty, kindliness, cheerfulness, and good manners. Theophrastus is interested primarily in social qualities, it is true, but the society he holds up to our view made its living mainly by mercantile pursuits, and many of his incidents are taken directly from the market place.

It is from the pages of the Attic orators, however, that we get the best idea of what an Athenian business man was like in the fourth century. Not only

conclussion

for

the Greeks

have we many fascinating sketches of
individuals — some good, some bad, as
is apt to be the case with individuals —
but numerous passages in which types
of conduct are approved or disapproved
show clearly what normal public opinion endorsed as 'good business' and what
it reprobated. The ideal business man
here put before us is not the clever,
unscrupulous sharper. He is the man
who conducts a factory or finances shipping ventures, year after year, without
ever having to come into a court of law
either as plaintiff or defendant; the
banker who earns the esteem and grati-
tude of his clients by serving them hon-
estly and aiding them in their difficulties;
the merchant who amasses a fortune by

fair dealing and makes liberal contribu-
tions in times of public distress for the
relief of those who have been less prosperous. The great thing in the world
of trade and finance, Demosthenes tells
us, is to combine diligence with honesty.

We have no reason to believe that
the difference between ideals of conduct
and actual practice was greater in ancient Athens than it is to-day. The relatively large amounts of capital needed
to carry on the trade in grain, so vital
to the very existence of the city, were
freely invested under a type of contract
in which the lender had no real security
save the personal integrity of the borrower; the latter was permitted to take
the money advanced him and voyage to

foreign parts, leaving behind him only his written engagement to repay. Credit had a large part in the transactions of the business world, and a responsible person apparently found little difficulty in procuring capital for operating a store, a factory, a mine, a bank, or any sort of legitimate business enterprise. The fact that the legal rate of interest on ordinary commercial loans was twelve per cent does not, as the modern reader might believe, point to an excessive moral risk. It indicates rather that the demand for commercial loans was active and the available supply of money limited, a very natural condition in the stage of industrial and commercial development Athens had reached in the fourth century. Profits were relatively large and quick, and money was well worth twelve per cent. The man who had no credit connections or could not afford to pay interest could generally raise money by organizing a mutual loan association among his friends; he paid no interest and gave no security, but his debt was a debt of honor, and not to repay meant shame and disgrace. Incredible as it may seem, this was a very usual way of securing capital, and, in my opinion, it speaks well for the Athenians. Bankers lent money upon real property and other kinds of security in the ordinary course of business, and a client could get a loan without security, by way of personal accommodation, just as he does to-day, or a loan for a friend upon his endorsement. Business at a bank, unlike most transactions in which money or property changed hands, generally went on without the formality of witnesses; the client trusted to the probity of his banker and to the accuracy of the entries in his books; a banker's accounts were accepted in a court of law as valid evidence of the transactions recorded. Ordinary buying and selling seem to have been conducted much as they are in a decent community nowadays, with no more formalities or legal safeguards than commonsense would dictate. Naturally we find occasional complaints of attempted extortion, but as a general rule fair prices on a basis of supply and demand seem to have prevailed, with very little governmental price-fixing. This was perhaps due in some measure to the Greek ability to control demand by doing without things; we moderns grumble at high prices, but—we pay. Nor can the existence in Athens of market commissioners and official inspectors of weights and measures be taken as evidence of a low moral standard in retail trade, for we ourselves are as yet unable to dispense with such functionaries as these.

It will, I trust, be apparent that the various conclusions I have laid before you are not intended as final and dogmatic affirmations, but are more in the nature of tentative and preliminary suggestions. The facts which we may regard as established are these: First, there has been little scientific inquiry into the economic life of ancient Greece, and none, practically, looking to determination of the moral principles upon which this economic life was based. The place which should be occupied in our economic histories by the results of such inquiry is taken by a congeries of assumptions. Secondly, these assumptions are not uncommonly founded on such misconceptions as were briefly discussed in our introduction. In the third place, I trust I have convinced you that our subject is well worth scientific study.

What I propose, then, is to substitute for this tissue of assumption, with which we have hitherto been content, a group of hypotheses to be studied and tested by scientific investigation. This obviously cannot be accomplished by the Hellenist unaided, nor yet by the economist, for these are problems on which economist and Hellenist must work together. It is my firm belief that the result of such scientific inquiry will be to demonstrate an essential unity in the various manifestations of what it is the fashion to call 'the Greek spirit.' As I have elsewhere said, the economic system of the Greeks, their finance, and the principles and ideals which underlie their business life, are just as truly an expression of the Greek genius as are the art and architecture, the literature, the science and philosophy, for which we are grateful to the age of Pericles.

THE END